PATSY ANN OF ALASKA

The True Story of a Dog

Tricia Brown

Illustrated by Jim Fowler

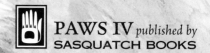
PAWS IV *published by*
SASQUATCH BOOKS

THE COLD, STEELY WATERS of the Inside Passage churned.
A great steamship was docking at Juneau, Alaska. Deep in the
ship's hold, a frightened puppy whimpered in its crate.

"Easy, girl. You're finally home." The steward massaged
the puppy's ears. His gentle touch calmed her when the loud
engines vibrated the ship's hull.

BY NIGHTFALL, the English bull terrier had a soft new bed at the dentist's house, and a new name as well: Patsy Ann.

Dr. Kaiser had twin daughters. Patsy Ann was their new baby. But Patsy Ann didn't want to be anybody's baby. The next day, she ran away to explore. Esther and Elizabeth called and called for her, but Patsy Ann didn't hear them.

SHE COULDN'T hear anything.

Patsy Ann was born deaf.

Patsy Ann saw a totem pole.

She smelled smoked salmon.

A friendly hand offered her some jerky.

She darted forward to steal a taste.

"BACK HOME AGAIN?" asked Mrs. Kaiser. It
was the third time neighbors had returned the
wandering dog.

"Maybe she doesn't like her bed," said Esther.

"Maybe she doesn't like us," said Elizabeth.

"Maybe she'll be happier somewhere else," said
their mother.

BUT PATSY ANN was just as restless at her next home.

The minister and his wife gave her treats and toys and lots of petting. Still she found ways to escape.

"I wonder why she doesn't come when we call her?" said Mrs. Rice. "Doesn't she want to be our dog?"

"Seems she's nobody's dog," said Reverend Rice. In time, they gave up trying to keep her, too.

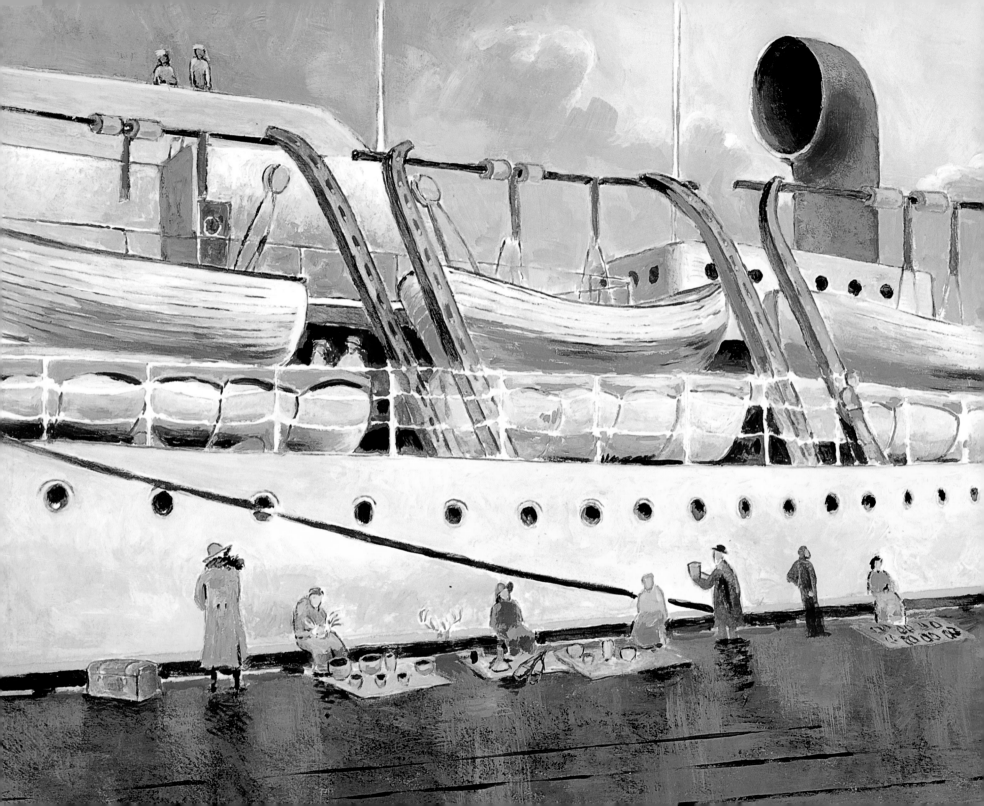

ONE DAY, Patsy Ann found her way down to the
crowded docks.

Giant steamships blasted their whistles.

Passengers poured down the gangplank.

Busy men rolled carts and heavy crates to
and from the ships.

Some dogs would have been scared by all that
hubbub, but not Patsy Ann.

A SHIP'S STEWARD gave Patsy Ann some scraps of steak. She edged closer and gobbled them greedily.

Patsy Ann was puzzled by this kindness, but when lunchtime came and the dockworkers shared their meatloaf sandwiches and cookies, she didn't turn them down. Patsy Ann liked the docks. There was food at the docks.

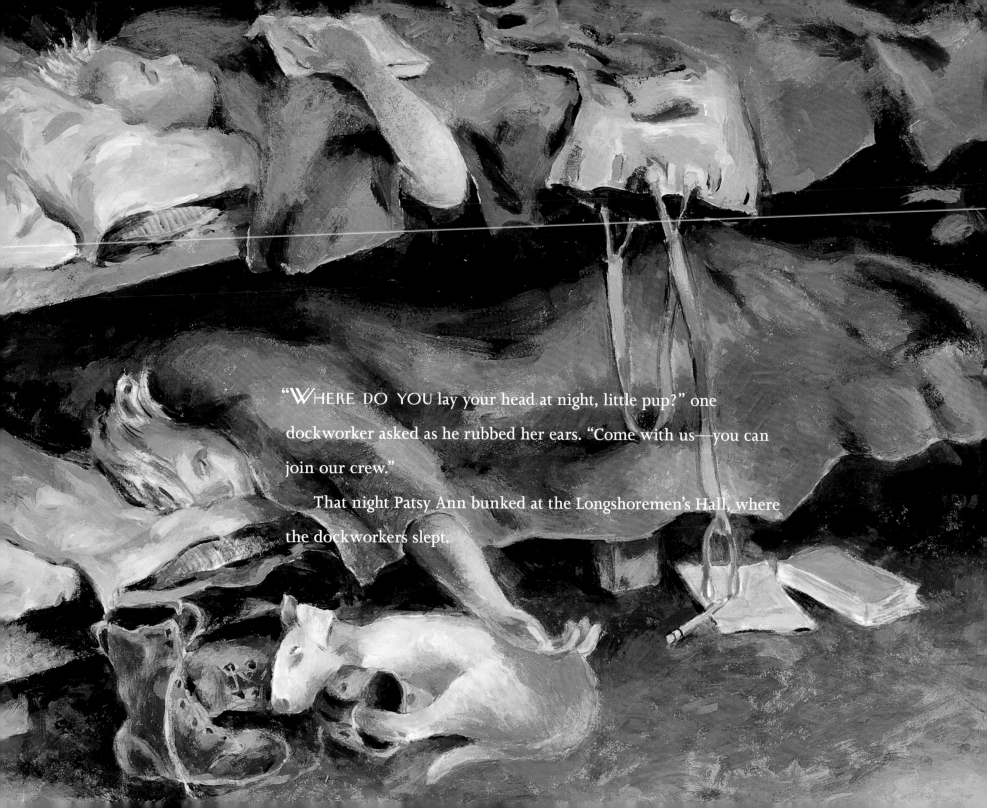

"WHERE DO YOU lay your head at night, little pup?" one
dockworker asked as he rubbed her ears. "Come with us—you can
join our crew."

That night Patsy Ann bunked at the Longshoremen's Hall, where
the dockworkers slept.

WHEN A NEW DAY DAWNED, Patsy Ann returned to the docks. While her friends moved cargo, she grinned at the passengers coming down the gangplank.

That's when Patsy Ann made a wonderful discovery.

All she had to do was squint her eyes and droop her ears, and she could get people to laugh and pet and feed her. She liked it very much.

"Oh, my, whose dog is that?" travelers asked, searching their pockets and purses for a treat.

"That's our new helper," the longshoremen called out. "Patsy Ann's in charge of greeting the ships."

SOON PATSY ANN came to the docks every time a new ship arrived. And every evening, she curled up in the Longshoremen's Hall. In time, the men began to think Patsy Ann was their dog. They even ordered a specially made leather collar with her name on it.

But Patsy Ann didn't appreciate the gift. It wasn't long before she used her feet to slip the collar off.

She was nobody's dog.

WHEN PATSY ANN wasn't sleeping at the Hall or visiting the docks, she happily roamed Juneau. At restaurants, tea parlors, and the pool hall, she squinted her eyes and drooped her ears to get pets and treats. As she wandered, she gathered more and more friends.

She walked the aisles of the theater while string musicians played Beethoven.

She warmed herself by the hotel's woodstove as gold miners swapped tall tales.

She pressed her paw prints in the fresh cement of a new sidewalk.

She stopped the Skagway-versus-Juneau baseball game when she stole the ball right off the field.

But whenever a ship steamed toward town, Patsy Ann stopped what she was doing and scampered to the docks to meet it, even before the captain blew the whistle.

"There goes Patsy Ann," the townspeople said. "Must be a ship coming in."

"How does she do that?" they asked each other. "I thought she was deaf."

"She must feel the engines vibrating the water."

"Or maybe she reads the ship schedule in the newspaper!"

PATSY ANN ALWAYS STOOD right at the bottom of the gangplank. As tourists filed off the ship, they laughed and petted her and took pictures of the little dog, ugly and cute at the same time, waiting just for them.

Stories about Patsy Ann began to spread outside of Juneau. A photographer sold postcards of Patsy Ann, and her picture went around the world in the mail.

Soon steamship passengers couldn't wait to dock at Juneau to meet Patsy Ann for themselves.

"Our Patsy Ann is the most famous dog west of the Mississippi!" the townspeople crowed.

YES, PATSY ANN WAS FAMOUS—but that didn't matter to the town dogcatcher. It was his job to catch any dog without a collar license. Patsy Ann's friends had bought one for her: once, twice, three times. But she had slipped out of each one.

One day, the dogcatcher spotted Patsy Ann headed for the port. He scooped her up in front of the hotel. Off went Patsy Ann to the pound.

Word spread through Juneau. The hotel desk clerk told the totem carver, who told a dockworker, who told the schoolteacher, who told the children, who told their parents. Pretty soon, just about everyone knew that Patsy Ann was stuck in "dog jail."

"IT CAN'T BE!" the grown-ups said. "This place isn't the same without her!"

"Free Patsy Ann!" children called out as they collected coins. "Free our town dog!"

SOON THE TOWNSPEOPLE had enough money to pay Patsy Ann's fine. A crowd of people brought it to City Hall. They wanted to talk to Mayor Goldstein.

"How can we make sure this won't happen again?" they asked.

"Patsy Ann wouldn't stay with the Kaisers," said the hotel clerk.

"And she wouldn't stay with the Rices," said the totem carver.

"And she wouldn't wear the collar we got her," said a longshoreman.

"Plus, we really missed her on the docks today!" declared a ship steward.

The mayor turned to the dogcatcher.

"But . . . but . . . she's *nobody's* dog!" he sputtered.

"No, sirree!" shouted the children. "Patsy Ann is *everybody's* dog!"

And everybody got noisy.

"PEOPLE, YOUR ATTENTION, PLEASE!" Mayor Goldstein called out. "I have an announcement!"

The crowd quieted down to listen.

"From this day forth, of all the dogs in our town, this one will never need a license. As a matter of fact, she works for the city now.

"I hereby proclaim Patsy Ann 'Official Boat Greeter of Juneau'!"

All the people cheered and clapped.

Patsy Ann sat right there at the mayor's feet, yet she didn't hear his proclamation or the wild cheering of her friends. But she didn't need to hear it to know that she was loved by the whole town.

Patsy Ann was truly everybody's dog.

This April 1935 photo is titled "The official greeter at Juneau." Patsy Ann's picture was taken on the docks when the USMS *North Star* arrived, carrying Midwest families en route to a New Deal experimental farming colony near Anchorage. *Alaska State Library, Mary Nan Gamble Collection, Willis T. Geisman, P270-056.*

REMEMBERING PATSY ANN

❧ October 12, 1929 to March 30, 1942 ❧

"[Patsy Ann] has a dingy white coat of her own, a mournful long face, and pathetic pink-rimmed eyes. Her figure is none too good, and as she sits with her ratlike tail stretched skimpily behind her, she looks like nobody's dog of particular lineage." —Daily Alaska Empire, 1933

PATSY ANN was a purebred English bull terrier who was born in Portland, Oregon, and was deaf from birth. She came to Juneau as a puppy at the start of the Great Depression and became famous as a one-dog welcoming committee on the Juneau docks, performing her job with distinction until her death. How Patsy Ann could "hear" the ships coming in before the rest of Juneau did always remained a mystery.

"Her name will live long after the names of some so-called important citizens of the world have been forgotten," wrote Juneau resident Carl Burrows in 1939, "for she is loved for herself, which is of the permanent kind of fame."

Patsy Ann was an old lady in dog years when she died quietly at the Longshoremen's Hall. Her friends gathered on the Alaska Steamship Company wharf to remember her antics and grieve together before her burial at sea. The whole community turned out to say good-bye to their town dog.

Fifty years later, in 1992, the Friends of Patsy Ann installed a bronze sculpture on the wharf in her honor. The statue of Patsy Ann sits facing the open waters of Gastineau Channel, as if she were watching for an incoming ship. Across one bronze paw is the expensive custom-made collar that was ordered by her longshoremen friends.

For hundreds of thousands of Juneau visitors, the statue is the first thing they see when they leave their cruise ships. Many stop and pose for a picture. The bronze is shiny from people petting her.

Many decades have passed, but Patsy Ann has earned "a permanent kind of fame," indeed.

For more about deafness in dogs, visit www.deafdogs.org.

For my dear aunt, Patricia Louise Parbs, and cousin,
Patricia Ann Burns, with love from Patsy —T.B.

For my sweet Cedar Lillyanny —J.F.

Printed in China by C&C Offset Printing Co. Ltd. Shenzhen,
 Guangdong Province, in November 2016
Published by Sasquatch Books
19 18 17   9 8 7 6

Editor: Michelle McCann
Cover and interior illustrations and layout: Jim Fowler
Cover design, interior design, and composition: Anna Goldstein

Library of Congress Cataloging-in-Publication Data is available.

ISBN-13: 978-1-57061-697-6 / ISBN-10: 1-57061-697-3

PAWS IV published by
Sasquatch Books
1904 Third Avenue, Suite 710
Seattle, WA 98101
(206) 467-4300
www.sasquatchbooks.com
custserv@sasquatchbooks.com

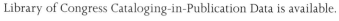